Play Gui

GW00467908

by Ulf Goran

LIST OF MELODIES

SWING IT JACOB

Melody: Traditional
Words: Kjell Åhslund
Translation: Paul Britten Austi

1:
(The boys)

Brother Jacob, wake up, Jacob!
Let it go, don't you know?
Have you gone to sleep, man,
Down there in the deep, man?
Swing it, man, swing it, man!

3:
(The boys)

Brother Jacob, wake up, Jacob!
Let's all shout, turn him out!
Are you nearly dead, man,
Or just gone to bed, man?
Swing it, man, swing it, man!

2:
(Jacob)

Dear old buddies, good old buddies,
Sure I hear you so clear,
Calling for me, but I
Need my little shut-eye.
Cool it down, cool it down!

4:
(Jacob)

Dear old buddies, good old buddies,
I'm OK, anyway.
Gotta sleep all night, man,
Then I'll be all right, man.
So just swing, ding dong ding.
(Ding dong ding, ding dong ding, etc)

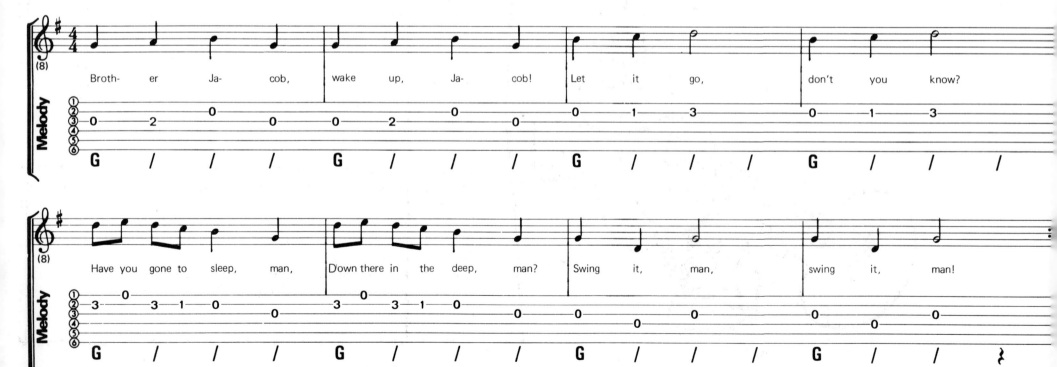

Choose your chord shape

G

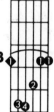

G

FOR MORE INFORMATION

See Accompaniment Guide and other special materials (details inside back cover).

THERE'S A HOLE IN MY BUCKET

Melody and words: Traditional
(Some new words by Ulf Göran Åhslund)

You'll find chord shapes to choose from on the previous page.

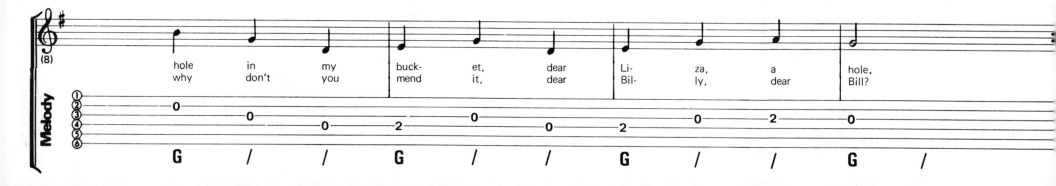

1 (Billy): There's a hole in my bucket, dear Liza, dear Liza,
There's a hole in my bucket, dear Liza, a hole.
  (Liza): Then why don't you mend it, dear Billy, dear Billy,
Then why don't you mend it, dear Billy, dear Bill?

2 (Billy): With what shall I mend it, dear Liza, dear Liza,
With what shall I mend it, dear Liza, with what?
  (Liza): With a straw you can mend it, dear Billy, dear Billy,
With a straw you can mend it, dear Billy, dear Bill.

3 (Billy): But the straw is too long, dear Liza, dear Liza,
But the straw is too long, dear Liza, too long.
  (Liza): Then why don't you cut it, dear Billy, dear Billy,
Then why don't you cut it, dear Billy, dear Bill?

4 (Billy): With what shall I cut it, dear Liza, dear Liza,
With what shall I cut it, dear Liza, with what?
  (Liza): With a knife you can cut it, dear Billy, dear Billy,
With a knife you can cut it, dear Billy, dear Bill.

5 (Billy): But the knife is too blunt, dear Liza, dear Liza,
But the knife is too blunt, dear Liza, too blunt.
  (Liza): Then why don't you whet it, dear Billy, dear Billy,
Then why don't you whet it, dear Billy, dear Bill?

6 (Billy): With what shall I whet it, dear Liza, dear Liza,
With what shall I whet it, dear Liza, with what?
  (Liza): With a stone you can whet it, dear Billy, dear Billy,
With a stone you can whet it, dear Billy, dear Bill?

7 (Billy): But the stone is too rough, dear Liza, dear Liza,
But the stone is too rough, dear Liza, too rough.
  (Liza): Then why don't you smooth it, dear Billy, dear Billy,
Then why don't you smooth it, dear Billy, dear Bill?

8 (Billy): With what shall I smooth it, dear Liza, dear Liza,
With what shall I smooth it, dear Liza, with what?
  (Liza): With water you'll smooth it, dear Billy, dear Billy,
With water you'll smooth it, dear Billy, dear Bill.

9 (Billy): How carry the water, dear Liza, dear Liza,
How carry the water, dear Liza, just how?
  (Liza): Why not use a bucket, dear Billy, dear Billy,
Why not use a bucket, dear Billy, dear Bill.?

10 (Billy): There's a hole in my bucket, dear Liza, dear Liza,
There's a hole in my bucket, dear Liza, a hole.
There's a hole in my bucket, dear Liza, a hole.
  (Liza): (spoken) Then mend it ...

Fret by fret table

The table below gives the name of each chord shape as it moves up the fingerboard fret by fret.

POSITION	SYMBOL	POSITION
1	F	
2	F♯ (G♭)	
3	G	
4	G♯ (A♭)	
5	A	
6	A♯ (B♭)	1
7	B	2
8	C	3
	C♯ (D♭)	4
	D	5
	D♯ (E♭)	6
	E	7
	F	8

FOR MORE INFORMATION

See Accompaniment Guide and other special materials (details inside back cover).

OH, SUSANNA

Melody and words: Stephen C. Foster

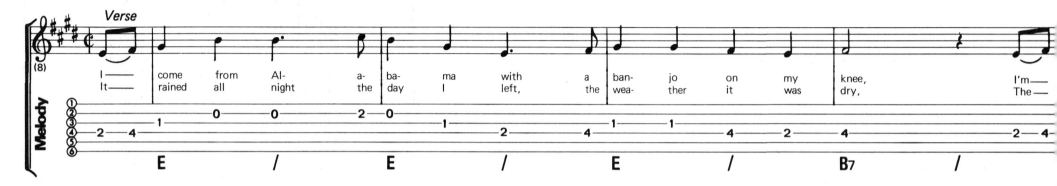

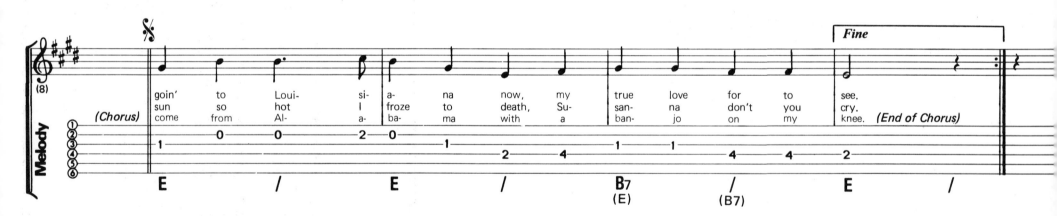

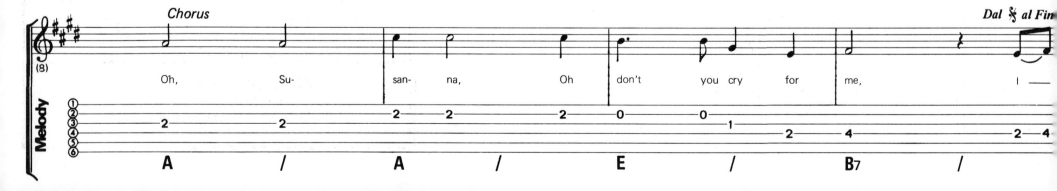

Verse 1: I come from Alabama with a banjo on my knee,
I'm goin' to Louisiana now, my true love for to see.
It rained all night the day I left, the weather it was dry,
The sun so hot I froze to death, Susanna don't you cry.

Chorus: Oh, Susanna, Oh don't you cry for me,
I come from Alabama with a banjo on my knee.

Verse 2: I had a dream the other night, when everything was still,
I dreamed I saw Susanna dear a-coming down the hill.
A red, red rose was in her cheek, a tear was in her eye,
I said to her, Susanna girl, Susanna don't you cry.

Chorus: Oh, Susanna, ...

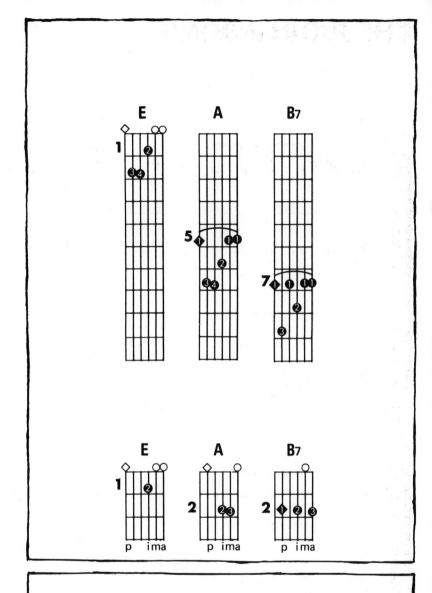

FOR MORE INFORMATION

See Accompaniment Guide and other special
materials (details inside back cover).

THE RIDDLE SONG

Melody and words: Traditional

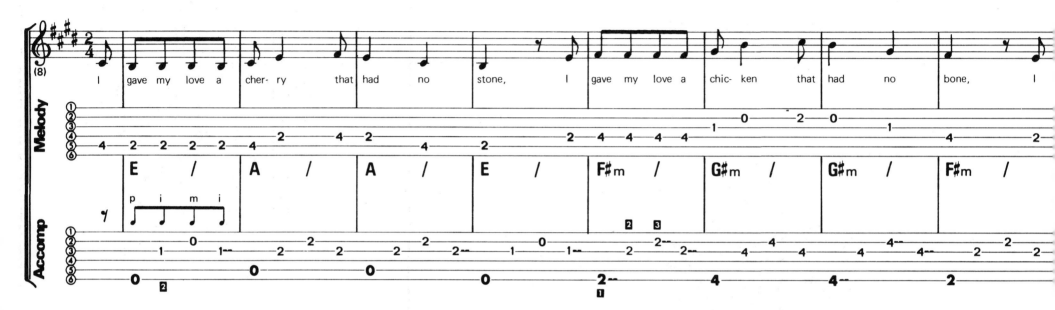

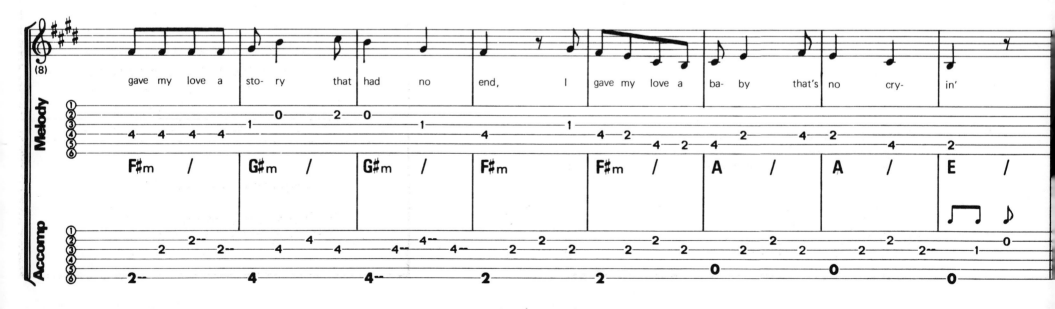

1: I gave my love a cherry that had no stone,
   I gave my love a chicken that had no bone,
   I gave my love a story that had no end,
   I gave my love a baby that's no cryin'.

2: How can there be a cherry that has no stone?
   How can there be a chicken that has no bone?
   How can there be a story that has no end?
   How can there be a baby that's no cryin'?

3: A cherry when it's bloomin', it has no stone,
   A chicken when it's peepin', it has no bone,
   The story that I love you, it has no end,
   A baby when it's sleepin', it's no cryin'.

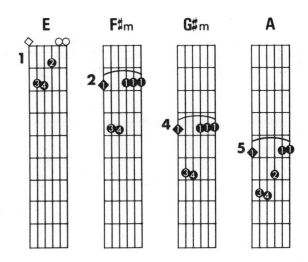

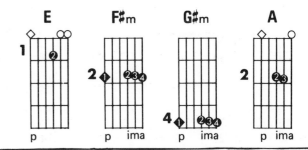

FOR MORE INFORMATION

See Accompaniment Guide and other special materials (details inside back cover).

IN THE WORLD THERE'S SOMEWHERE

Melody: Ulf Göran Åhslund
Words: Ulf Göran Åhslund & Paul Britten Aus...

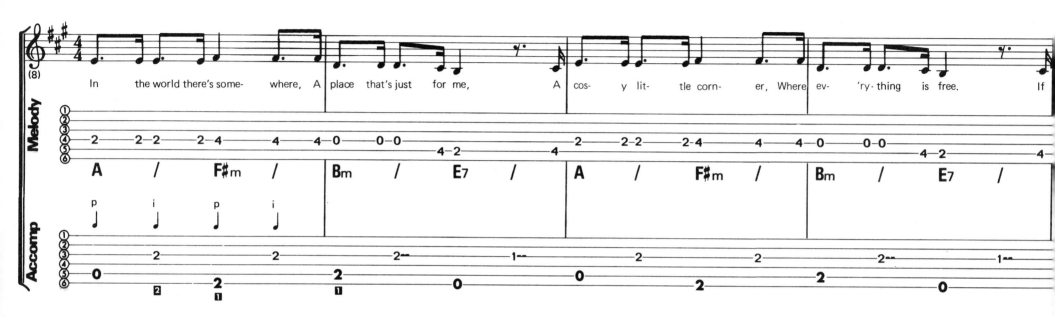

In the world there's some- where, A place that's just for me, A cos- y lit- tle corn- er, Where ev- 'ry-thing is free. If

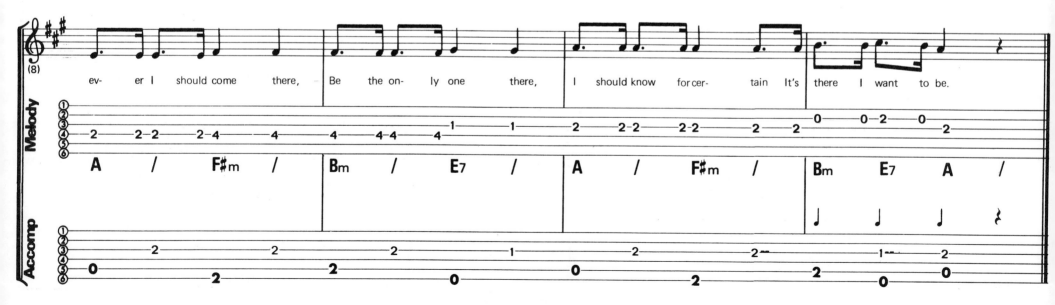

ev- er I should come there, Be the on- ly one there, I should know for cer- tain It's there I want to be.

1: In the world there's somewhere,
A place that's just for me,
A cosy little corner,
Where ev'rything is free.
If ever I should come there,
Be the only one there.
I should know for certain
It's there I want to be.

2: In the world there's someone,
A one that's just for me,
A heart I can rely on
That's beating wild and free.
If ever I should find it,
I would never bind it,
I'd be just as happy
So long it beats for me.

3: In the world there's somewhere,
A place where we can be,
A cosy little corner,
Where ev'rything is free.
I'm asking you to come there
'Cause you do belong there.
Can't you be my loved one
And share it all with me?

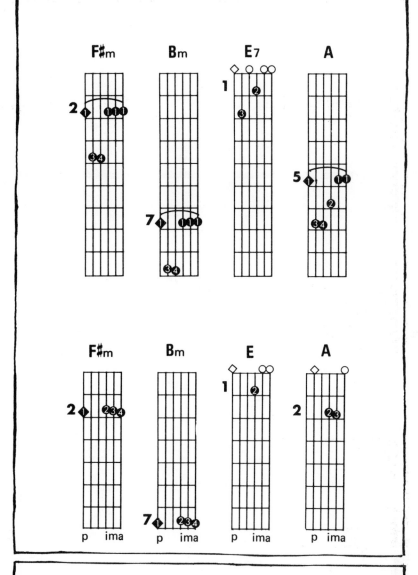

FOR MORE INFORMATION

See Accompaniment Guide and other special materials (details inside back cover).

HE'S GOT THE WHOLE WORLD IN HIS HANDS

Melody and words: Tradition

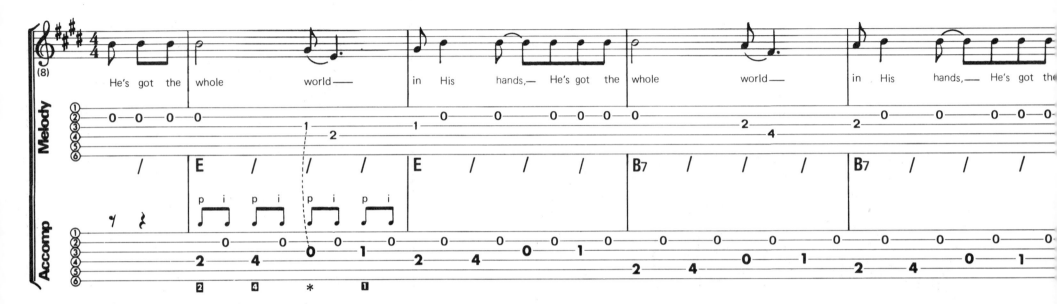

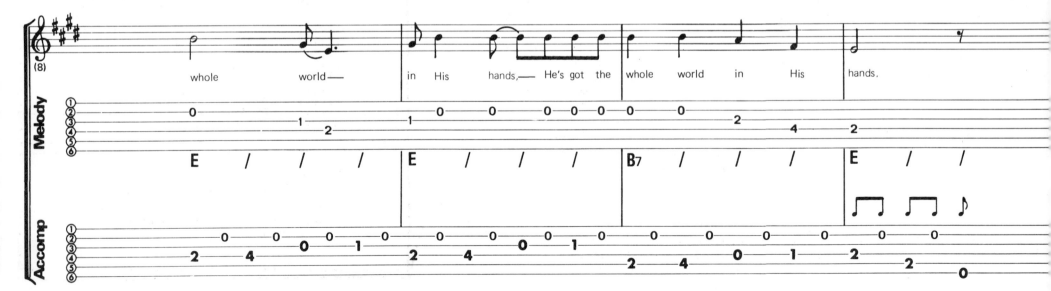

* The accomp's G-natural against the melody's G-sharp produces a so-called 'blues' effect.

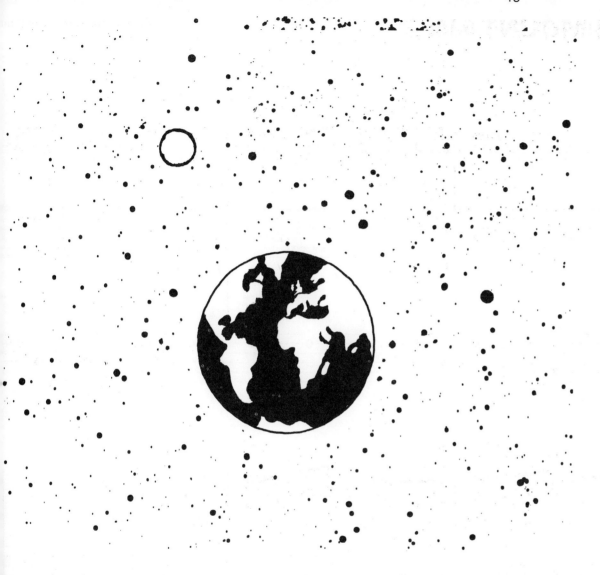

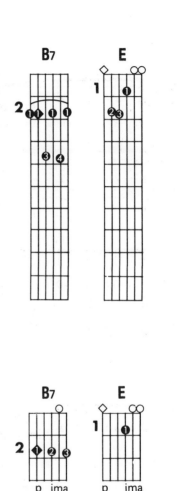

He's got the whole world in His hands,
He's got the whole world in His hands,
He's got the whole world in His hands,
He's got the whole world in His hands.

He's got the wind and the rain in His hands,
He's got the wind and the rain in His hands,
He's got the wind and the rain in His hands,
He's got the whole world in His hands.

3: He's got the tiny little baby in His hands,
He's got the tiny little baby in His hands,
He's got the tiny little baby in His hands,
He's got the whole world in His hands.

4: He's got you and me in His hands,
He's got you and me in His hands,
He's got you and me in His hands,
He's got the whole world in His hands.

FOR MORE INFORMATION

See Accompaniment Guide and other special materials (details inside back cover).

SHE'LL BE COMIN' 'ROUND THE MOUNTAIN

Melody and words: Tradition

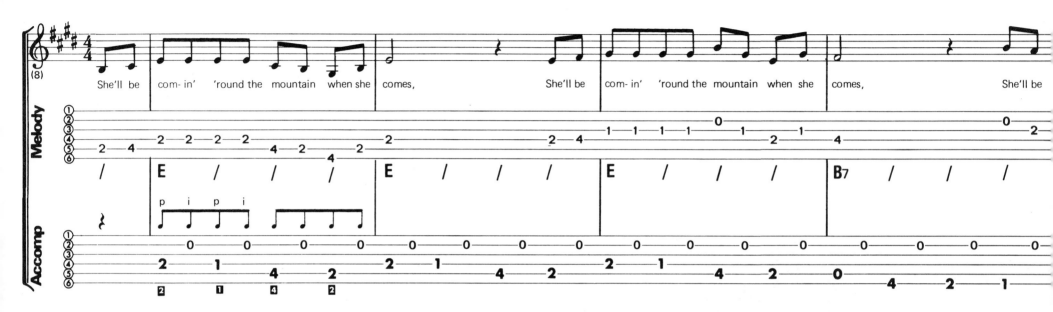

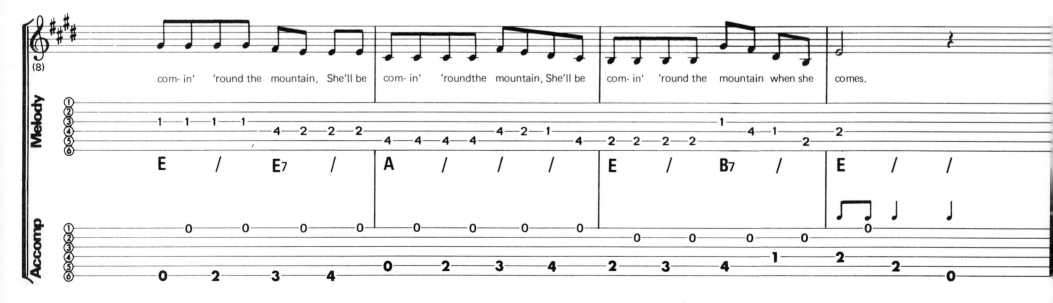

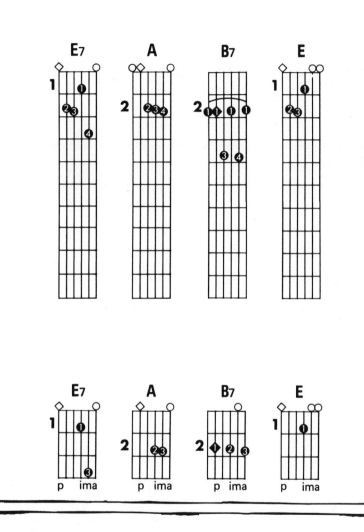

She'll be comin' 'round the mountain when she comes,
She'll be comin' 'round the mountain when she comes,
She'll be comin' 'round the mountain,
She'll be comin' 'round the mountain,
She'll be comin' 'round the mountain when she comes.

She'll be drivin' six white horses when she comes,
She'll be drivin' six white horses when she comes,
She'll be drivin' six white horses,
She'll be drivin' six white horses,
She'll be drivin' six white horses when she comes.

Oh, we'll all go out to meet her when she comes,
Oh, we'll all go out to meet her when she comes,
We will kill the old red rooster,
We will kill the old red rooster,
And we'll all have chicken dumplins when she comes.

FOR MORE INFORMATION

See Accompaniment Guide and other special materials (details inside back cover).

YES, MY DARLING DAUGHTER

Music and words:
Jack Lawrence and Albert Sirma

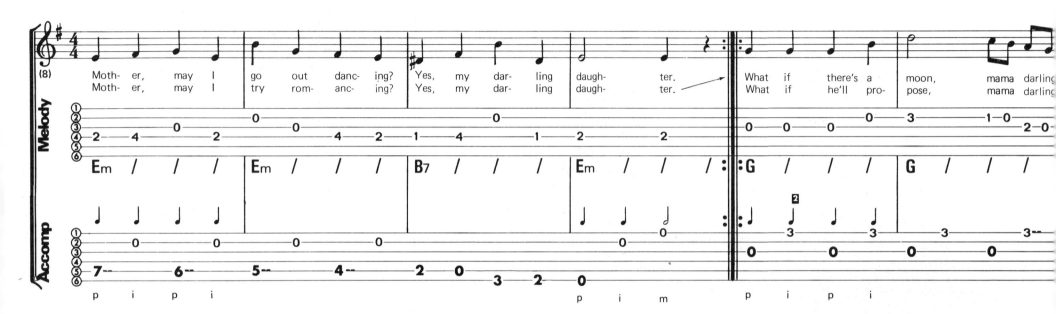

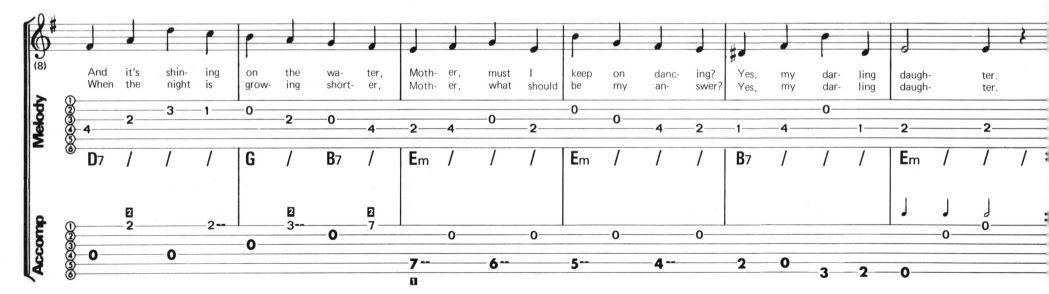

Melody and words used by permission of Chappell & Co. Ltd.

Mother, may I go out dancing?
Yes, my darling daughter.
Mother, may I try romancing?
Yes, my darling daughter.
What if there's a moon, mama darling,
And it's shining on the water,
Mother, must I keep on dancing?
Yes, my darling daughter.
What if he'll propose, mama darling,
When the night is growing shorter,
Mother, what should be my answer?
Yes, my darling daughter.

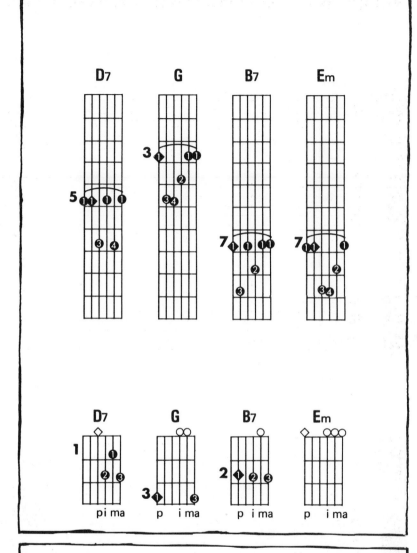

FOR MORE INFORMATION

See Accompaniment Guide and other special materials (details inside back cover).

DOWN BY THE RIVERSIDE

Melody and words: Traditional

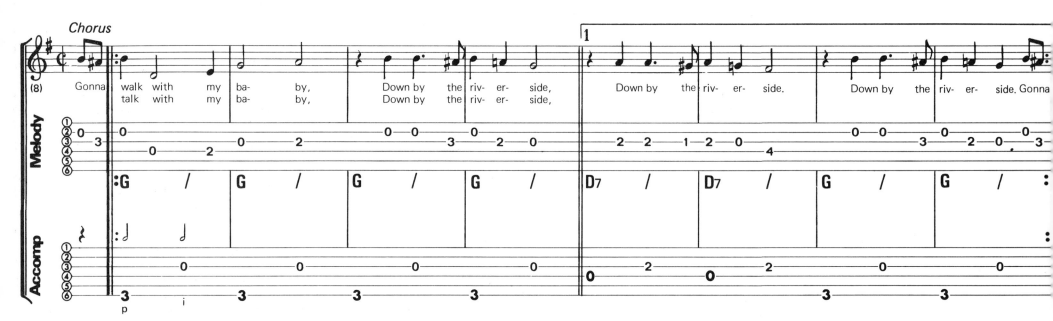

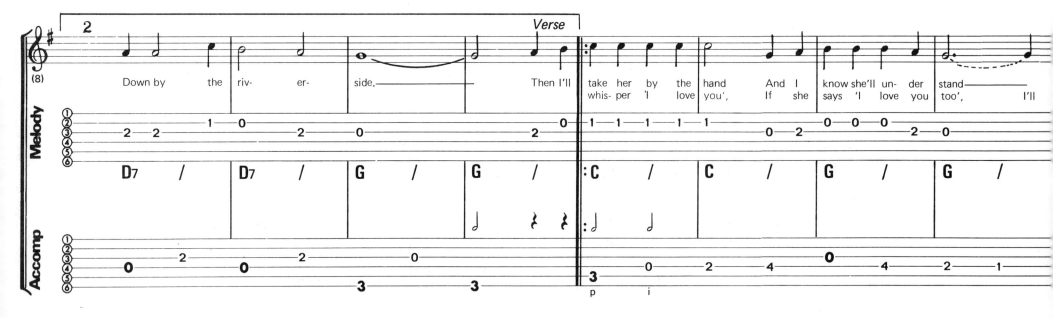

Chorus 1: Gonna walk with my baby,
Down by the riverside,
Down by the riverside,
Down by the riverside.
Gonna talk with my baby,
Down by the riverside,
Down by the riverside.

Verse: Then I'll take her by the hand
And I'll know she'll understand
Just what I have to say,
When I whisper 'I love you',
If she says 'I love you too',
I'll ask her to name the day.

Chorus 2: Then I'll carry my baby,
Down by the riverside,
Down by the riverside,
Down by the riverside.
And I'll marry my baby,
Down by the riverside,
Down by the riverside.

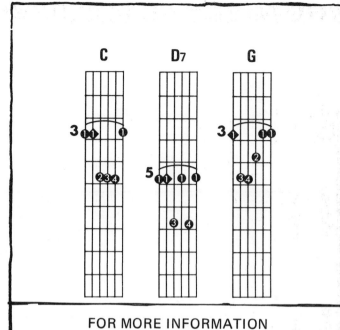

FOR MORE INFORMATION

See Accompaniment Guide and other special materials (details inside back cover).

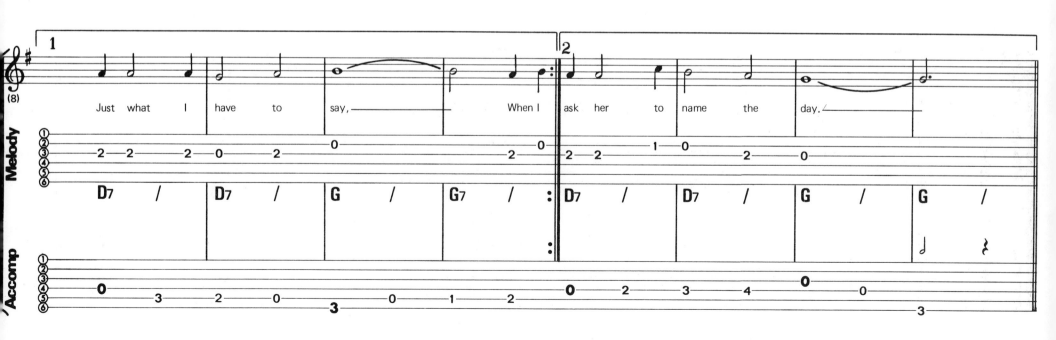

THE FOGGY FOGGY DEW

Melody and words: Traditiona

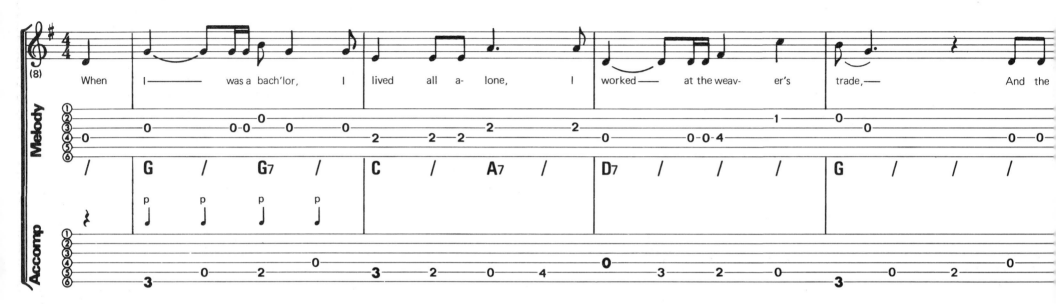

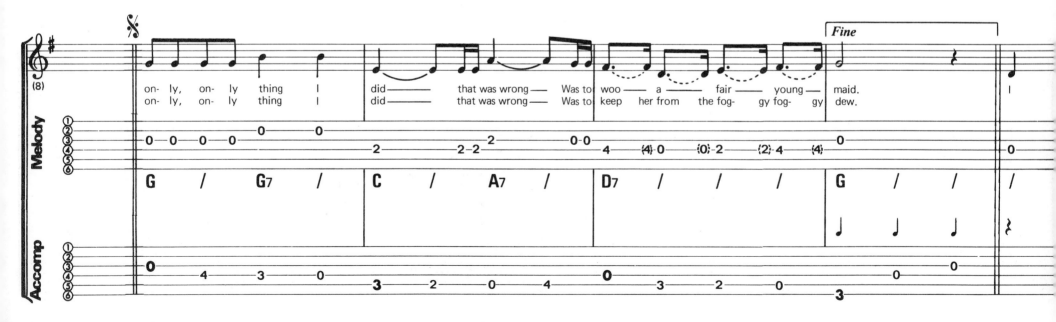

1: When I was a bach'lor, I lived all alone,
I worked at the weaver's trade,
And the only, only thing I did that was wrong
Was to woo a fair young maid.
I wooed her in the wintertime
And in the summer too:
And the only, only thing I did that was wrong
Was to keep her from the foggy foggy dew.

2: One night she knelt close by my side,
When I was fast asleep:
She threw her arms around my neck
And then began to weep.
She wept, she cried, she tore her hair,
Ah me, what could I do?
So all night long I held her in my arms,
Just to keep her from the foggy foggy dew.

3 Oh, I am a bach'lor, I live with my son,
We work at the weaver's trade:
And ev'ry single time I look into his eyes
He reminds me of a fair young maid.
He reminds me of the wintertime
And of the summer too:
And the many, many times that I held her in my arms,
Just to keep her from the foggy foggy dew.

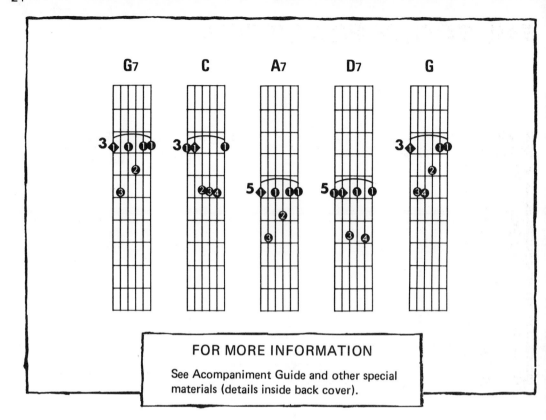

FOR MORE INFORMATION

See Acompaniment Guide and other special materials (details inside back cover).

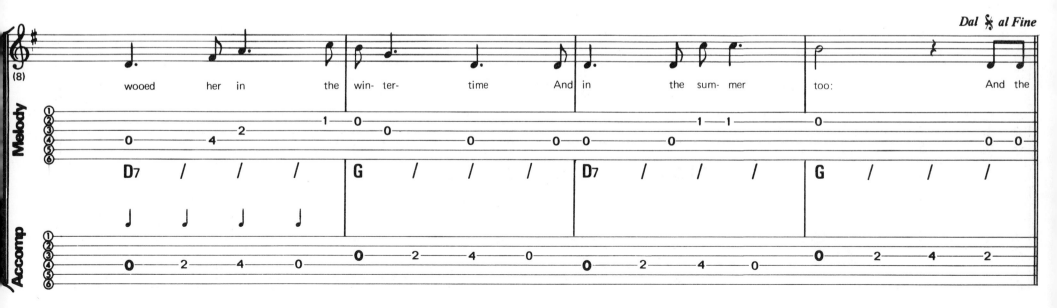

OH, NO JOHN

Melody and words: Traditional

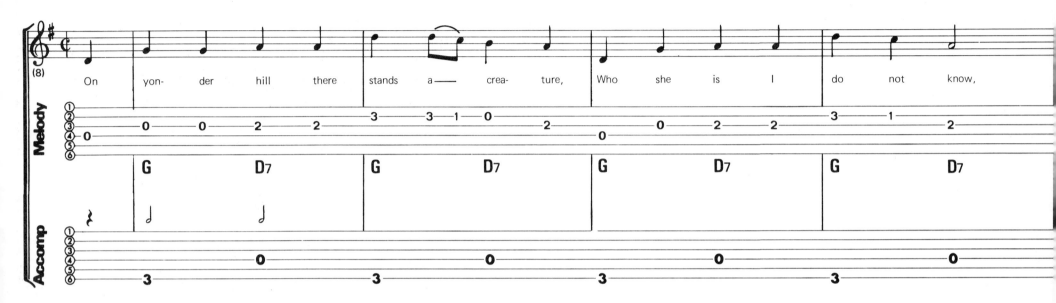

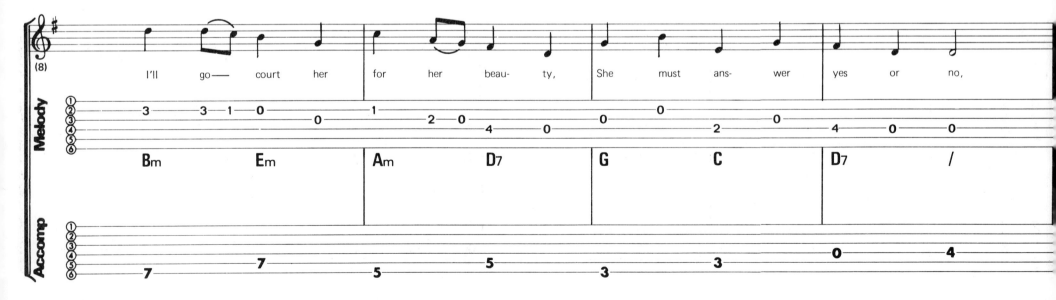

: On yonder hill there stands a creature,
Who she is I do not know,
I'll go court her for her beauty,
She must answer yes or no,
'Oh, no John, no John, no John, no!'

: My father was a Spanish captain,
Went to sea a month ago.
First he kissed me, then he left me,
Bade me always answer no,
'Oh, no John, no John, no John, no!'

: Oh, madam, I will give you jewels,
I will make you rich and free,
I will give you gold and silver,
Madam, if you'll marry me,
'Oh, no John, no John, no John, no!'

4: Your lips are like the rosebud blooming,
And your bosom's white as snow,
In your chamber there is treasure,
May I view it, yes or no?
'Oh, no John, no John, no John, no!'

5: Oh, madam, since you are so cruel,
And you wish to scorn me so,
If I may not be your lover,
Madam, will you let me go?
'Oh, no John, no John, no John, no!'

6: Oh, hark, I hear the church bells ringing,
Will you come and be my wife,
Or, dear madam, have you settled,
To live single all your life?
'Oh, no John, no John, no John, no!'

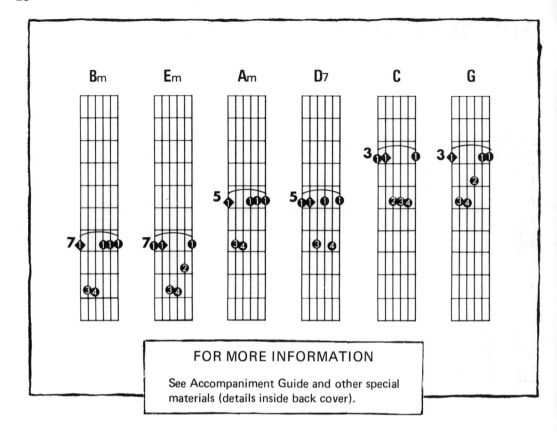

FOR MORE INFORMATION

See Accompaniment Guide and other special materials (details inside back cover).

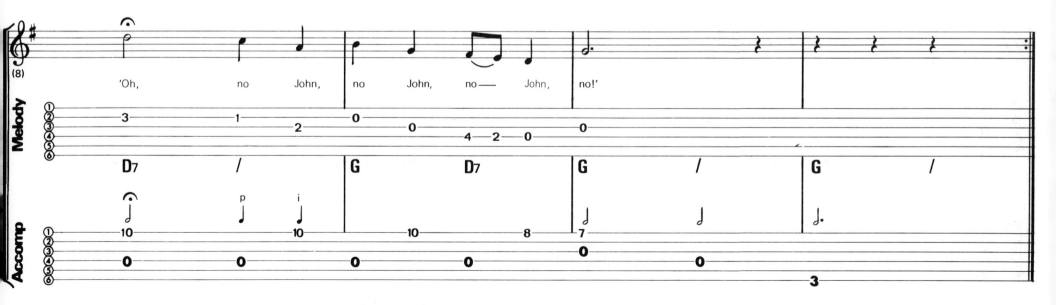

JOHNNY, I HARDLY KNEW YE!

Melody and words: Traditional

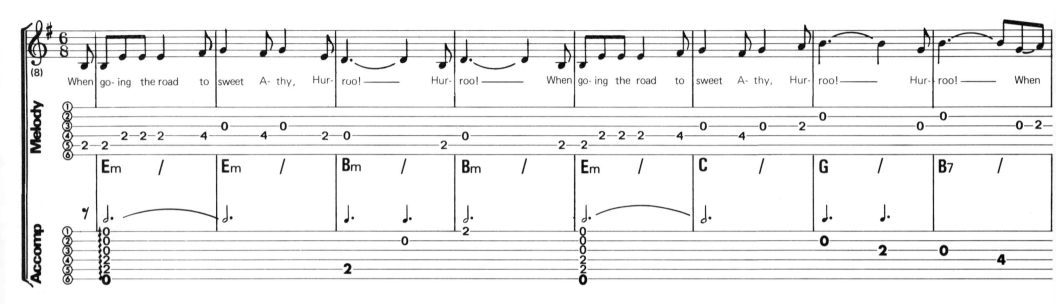

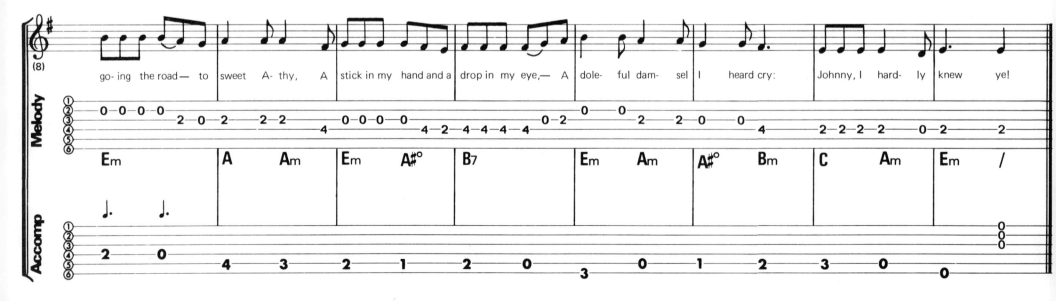

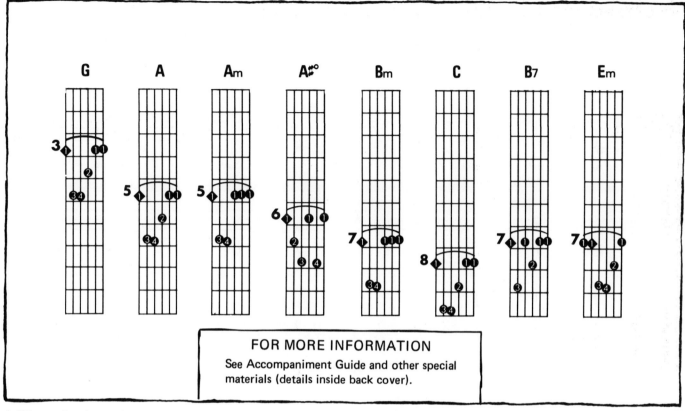

FOR MORE INFORMATION
See Accompaniment Guide and other special materials (details inside back cover).

1: When going the road to sweet Athy, Hurroo! Hurroo!
When going the road to sweet Athy, Hurroo! Hurroo!
When going the road to sweet Athy,
A stick in my hand and a drop in my eye,
A doleful damsel I heard cry:
Johnny, I hardly knew ye!

2: With your drums and guns and guns and drums, Hurroo! Hurroo!
With your drums and guns and guns and drums, Hurroo! Hurroo!
With your drums and guns and guns and drums
The enemy nearly slew ye.
O, darling dear, you look so queer.
Faith Johnny, I hardly knew ye!

3: Where are your eyes that look'd so mild, Hurroo! Hurroo!
Where are your eyes that look'd so mild, Hurroo! Hurroo!
Where are your eyes that look'd so mild
When my heart you so beguil'd.
Why did you skedaddle from me and the child?
Why Johnny, I hardly knew ye!

4: Where are the legs with which you run, Hurroo! Hurroo!
Where are the legs with which you run, Hurroo! Hurroo!
Where are the legs with which you run
When you went for to carry a gun.
Indeed your dancing days are done.
Faith Johnny, I hardly knew ye!

5: I'm happy for to see you home, Hurroo! Hurroo!
I'm happy for to see you home, Hurroo! Hurroo!
I'm happy for to see you home
All from the Islands of Ceylon
So low in flesh, so high in bone.
Faith Johnny, I hardly knew ye!

LAURA LEE

Words and melody, based on a
traditional song, by Ulf Göran Åhslund
and William Clauson

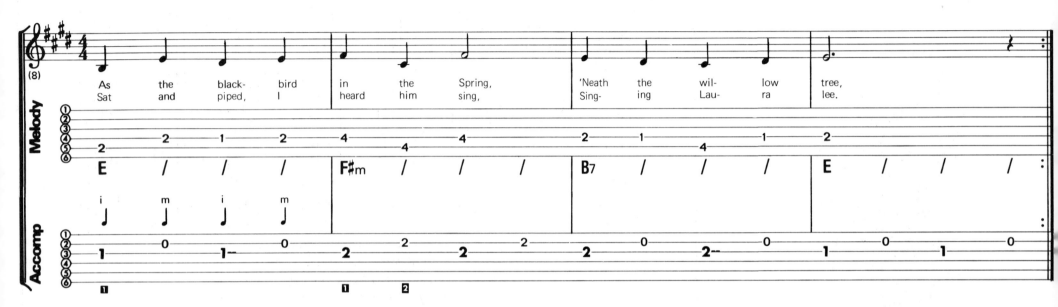

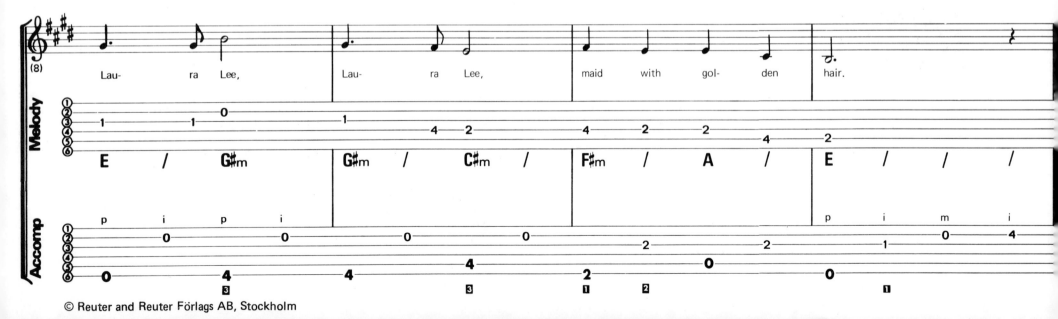

© Reuter and Reuter Förlags AB, Stockholm

1: As the blackbird in the Spring,
   'Neath the willow tree,
   Sat and piped, I heard him sing,
   Singing Laura Lee.
   Laura Lee, Laura Lee, maid with golden hair.
   Sunshine came along with thee, and swallows in the air.

2: In thy blush the rose was born,
   Music when you spake.
   Through thine azure eye the moon
   Sparkling seemed to break.
   Laura Lee, Laura Lee, birds of crimson wing,
   Never song have sung to me as in that bright sweet Spring.

3: When the mistletoe was green
   'Midst the Winter snows,
   Sunshine in thy face was seen
   Kissing lips of rose.
   Laura Lee, Laura Lee, makes the sad heart sing,
   Love and light return with thee, and swallows in the Spring.

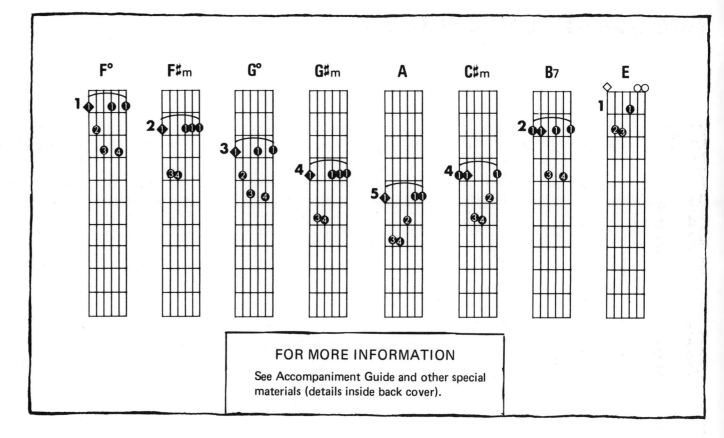

FOR MORE INFORMATION

See Accompaniment Guide and other special materials (details inside back cover).

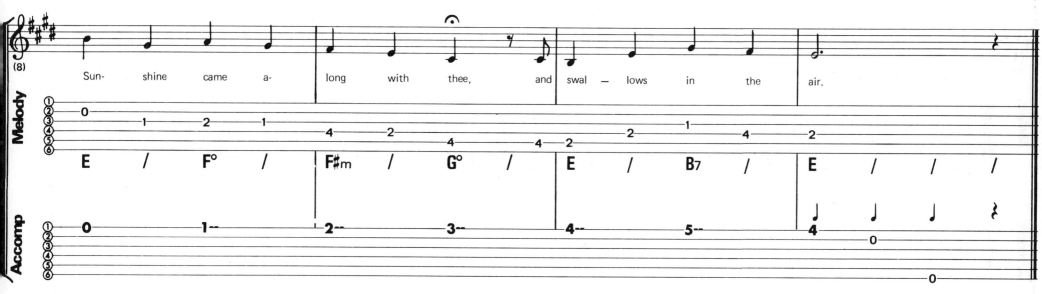

THE CAMPTOWN RACES

Melody and words: Stephen C. Foster

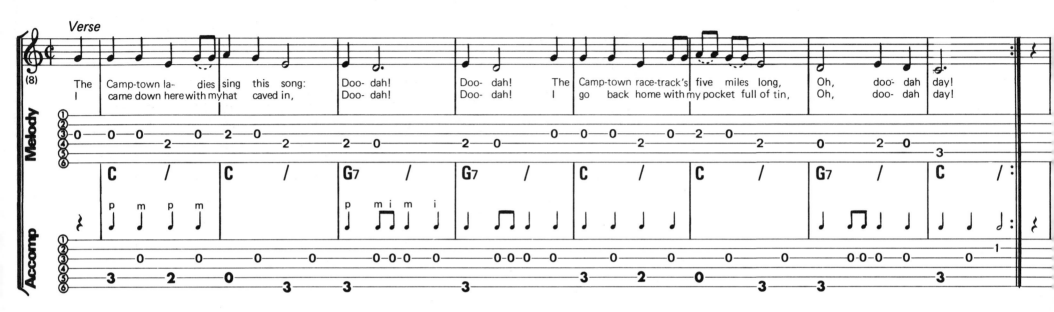

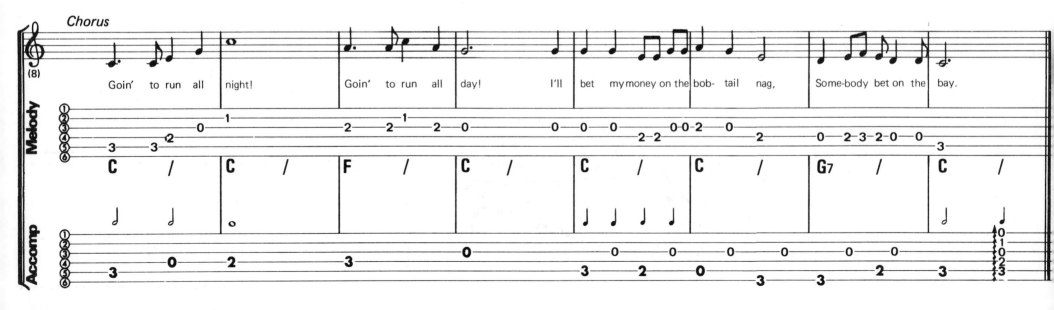

Verse 1: The Camptown ladies sing this song:
Doodah! Doodah!
The Camptown race-track's five miles long,
Oh, doodah day!
I came down there with my hat caved in,
Doodah! Doodah!
I go back home with my pocket full of tin,
Oh, doodah day!

Chorus: Goin' to run all night!
Goin' to run all day!
I'll bet my money on the bob-tail nag,
Somebody bet on the bay.

Verse 2: The long-tail filly and the big black hoss,
Doodah! Doodah!
They fly the track and they both cut across,
Oh, doodah day!
The blind hoss stickin' in a big mud hole,
Doodah! Doodah!
Can't touch the bottom with a ten-foot pole,
Oh, doodah day!

Chorus: Goin' to run ...

Verse 3: Old muley cow came on the track,
Doodah! Doodah!
The bob-tail flung her over his back,
Oh, doodah day!
Then flew along like a railroad car,
Doodah! Doodah!
Runnin' a race with a shootin' star,
Oh, doodah day!

Chorus: Goin' to run ...

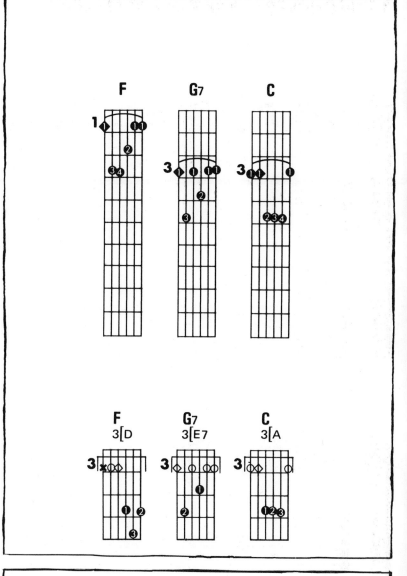

FOR MORE INFORMATION

See Accompaniment Guide and other special materials (details inside back cover).

MIDNIGHT IN MOSCOW

Traditional

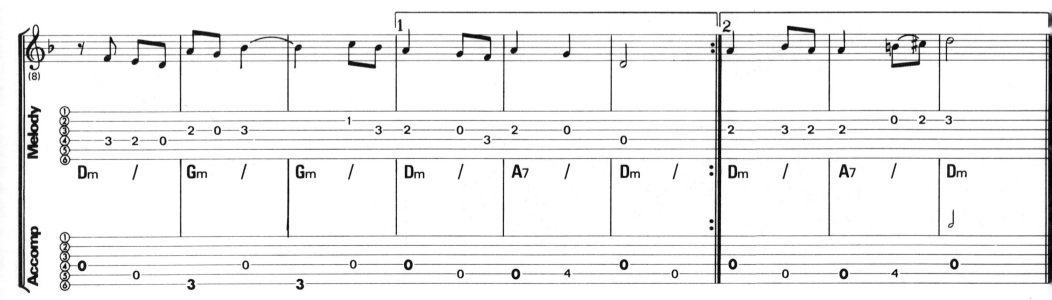

Melody used by permission of Tyler Music Ltd.

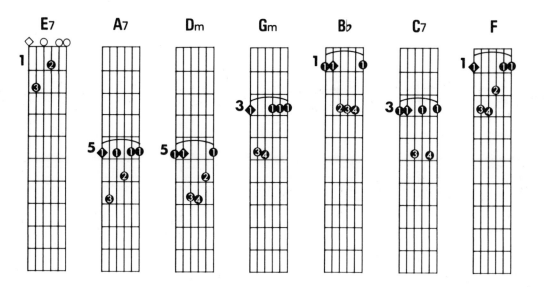

If you like, you can use the "coloured" chords, below, instead of the "pure" major, minor and seventh's, above.

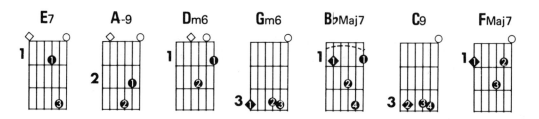

FOR MORE INFORMATION

See Accompaniment Guide and other special materials (details inside back cover).

WHERE HAVE ALL THE FLOWERS GONE?

Melody and words: Pete Seeger

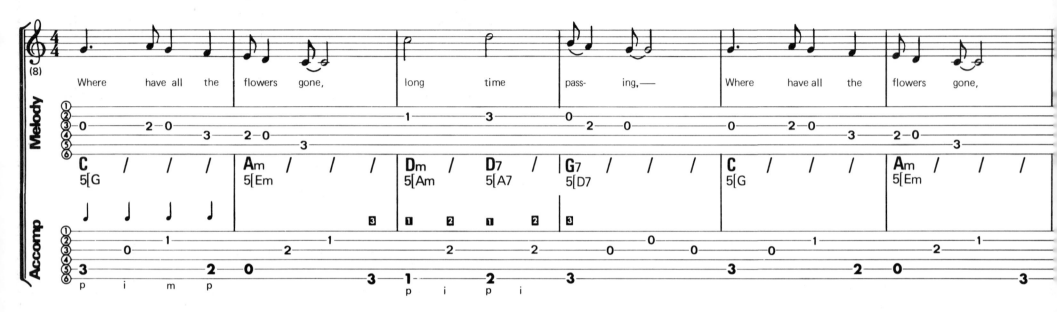

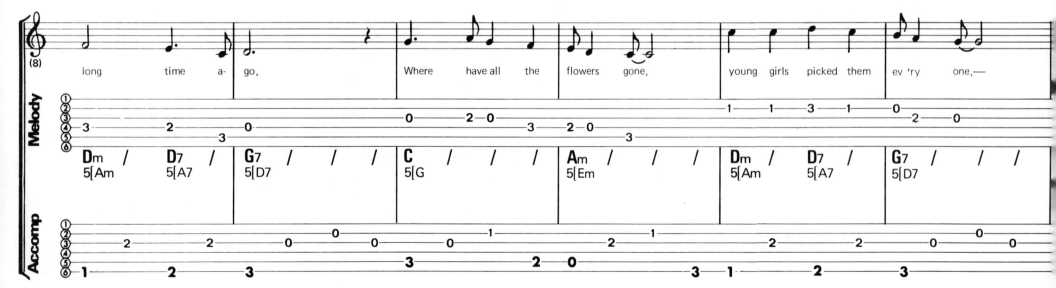

Melody and words used by permission of Harmony Music Ltd.

: Where have all the flowers gone, long time passing,
Where have all the flowers gone, long time ago,
Where have all the flowers gone, young girls picked them every one,
When will they ever learn, when will they ever learn?

: Where have all the young girls gone, long time passing,
Where have all the young girls gone, long time ago,
Where have all the young girls gone, gone to young men every one,
When will they ever learn, when will they ever learn?

: Where have all the young men gone, long time passing,
Where have all the young men gone, long time ago,
Where have all the young men gone, they are all in uniform,
When will they ever learn, when will they ever learn?

: Where have all the soldiers gone, long time passing,
Where have all the soldiers gone, long time ago,
Where have all the soldiers gone, gone to graveyards every one,
When will they ever learn, when will they ever learn?

: Where have all the graveyards gone, long time passing,
Where have all the graveyards gone, long time ago,
Where have all the graveyards gone, covered with flowers every one,
When will they ever learn, when will they ever learn?

: Where have all the flowers gone, etc.

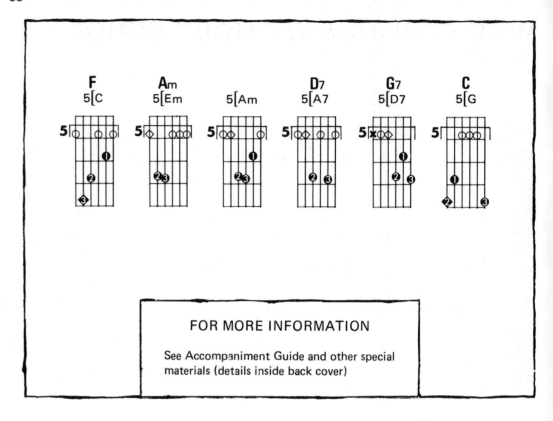

FOR MORE INFORMATION

See Accompaniment Guide and other special
materials (details inside back cover)

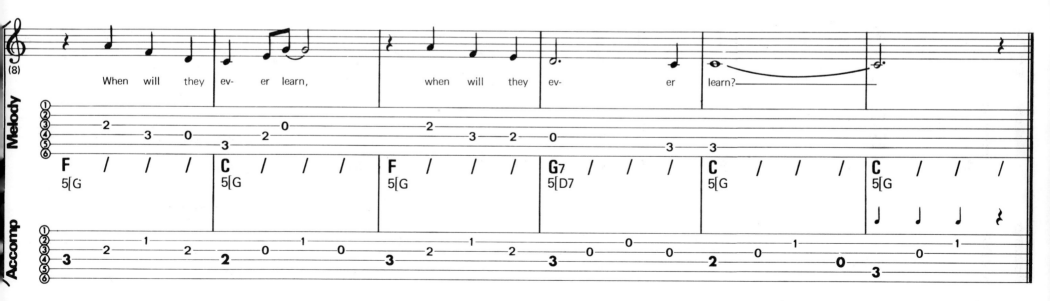

WHO CAN SAIL WITHOUT WIND?

Melody line and tablature accompaniment

Traditional song from Finland
English words by Ulf Göran Åhslund

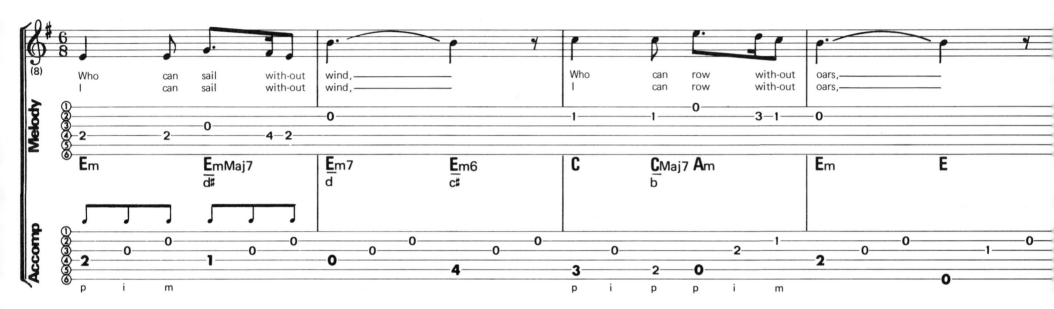

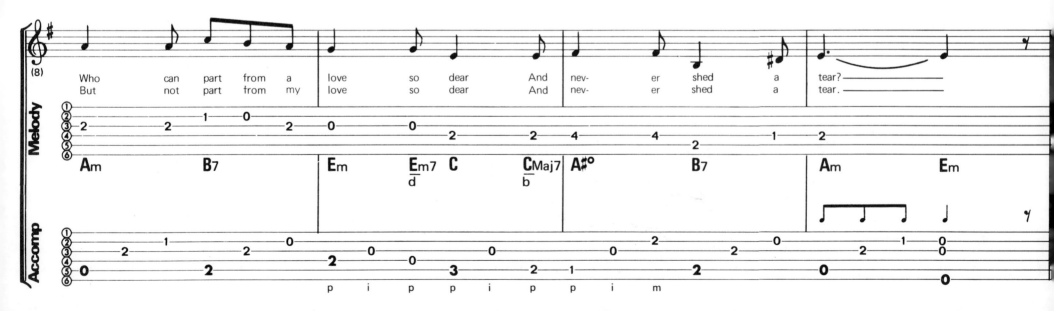

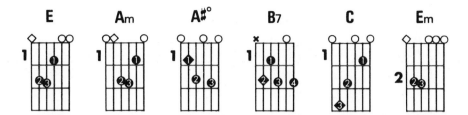

E   Am   A#°   B7   C   Em

FOR MORE INFORMATION

See Accompaniment Guide and other special materials (details inside back cover).

DO THE SAME AS ME... SWITCH TO AND FRO BETWEEN THE ACCOMPS ON THESE TWO PAGES AND COMPARE THE EFFECTS...

WHO CAN SAIL WITHOUT WIND?

Chord accompaniment

Extra marks, to help you divide up the text.

6/8

‖: Em / / / / / |Em / / / / / |
Who----- can-- sail --with-out --- wind,- - - - - - - - - - - -

| C / / Am / / |Em / / E / / |
Who------ can-- row--with-out--- oars,- - - - - - - - - - -

| Am / / B7 / / |Em / / C / / |
Who----- can-- part-from a ----love ----- so -- dear   And

| A#° / / B7 / / |Am / / Em / / :‖
nev - - - - - er --- shed --- a - - - tear?- - - - - - - - - - -

1: Who can sail without wind,
   Who can row without oars,
   Who can part from a love so dear
   And never shed a tear?

2: I can sail without wind,
   I can row without oars,
   But not part from my love so dear
   And never shed a tear.

THE STREETS OF LAREDO

Melody and words: Traditional
(Some new words by Ulf Göran Åhslund)

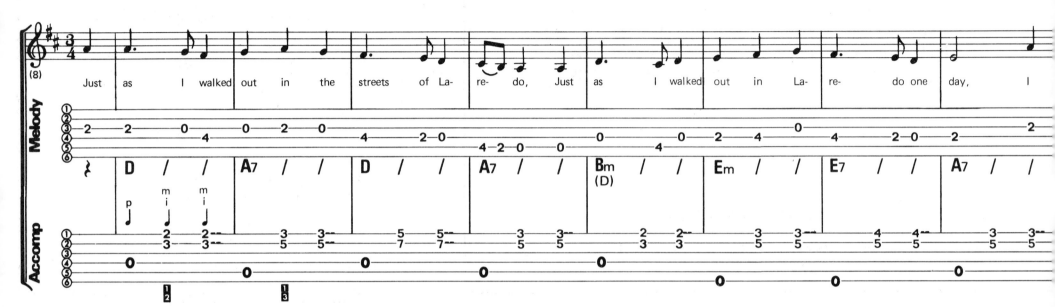

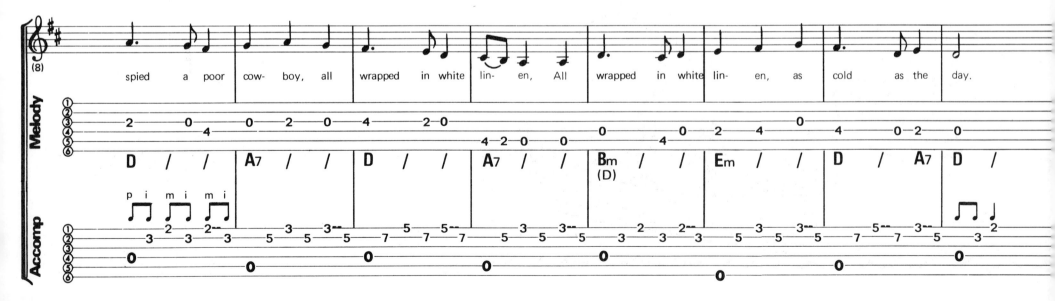

: Just as I walked out in the streets of Laredo,
Just as I walked out in Laredo one day,
I spied a poor cowboy, all wrapped in white linen,
All wrapped in white linen, as cold as the day.

: 'I see by your outfit that you are a cowboy,'
These words he did say as I boldly stepped by,
'Come sit here beside me and hear my sad story,
I'm shot in the breast and I know I must die.'

: 'Get six jolly cowboys to carry my coffin,
Get six pretty maidens to carry my pall:
Put bunches of roses all over my coffin,
Red roses to deaden the clods as they fall.'

: 'Oh, beat the drum slowly and play the fife lowly,
Oh, play the dead march as I'm carried along,
When down in the valley you lay the sod over me,
Oh, I am so young but I know I've done wrong.'

: We beat the drum slowly and played the fife lowly,
And bitterly wept as we bore him along:
So young and so handsome and ending so bravely,
We all loved the cowboy although he'd done wrong.

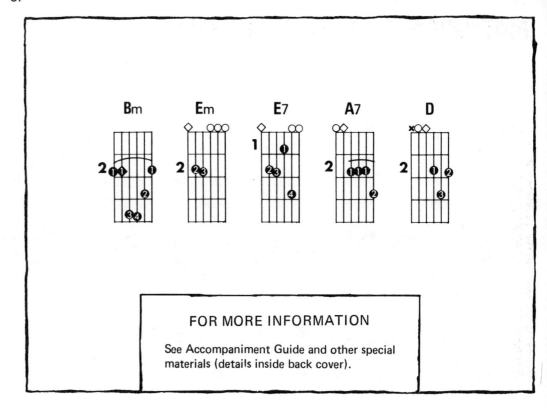

FOR MORE INFORMATION

See Accompaniment Guide and other special materials (details inside back cover).

Ad. lib.: Prelude, postlude, and interlude

ARIETTA

Guitar Solo by Joseph Küffner
Arrangement for guitar and recorder
(or other melody instrument) by Ulf Göran Åhslund

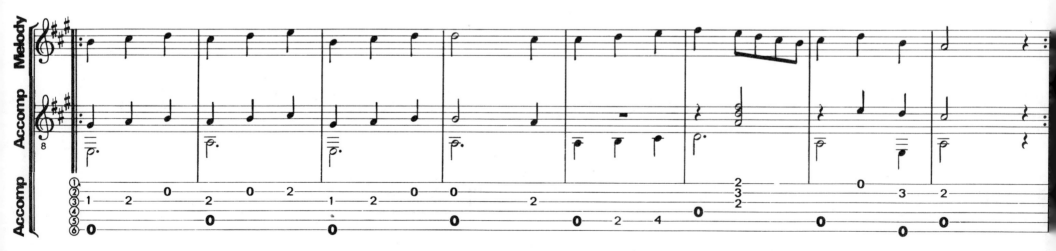

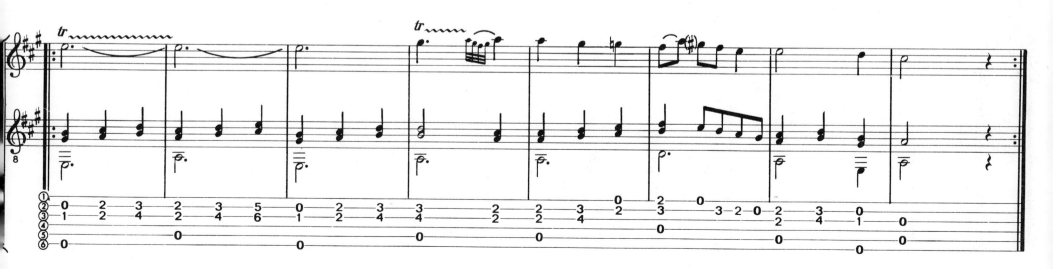

EARLY MORNIN' RAIN

'Melody and words: Gordon Lightfoo[t]

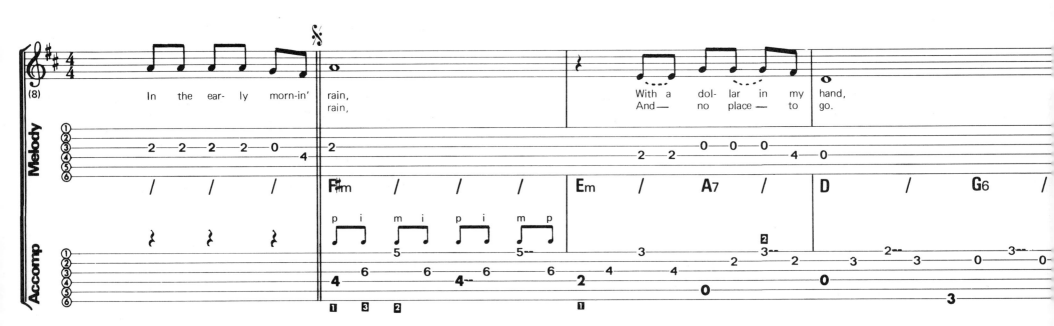

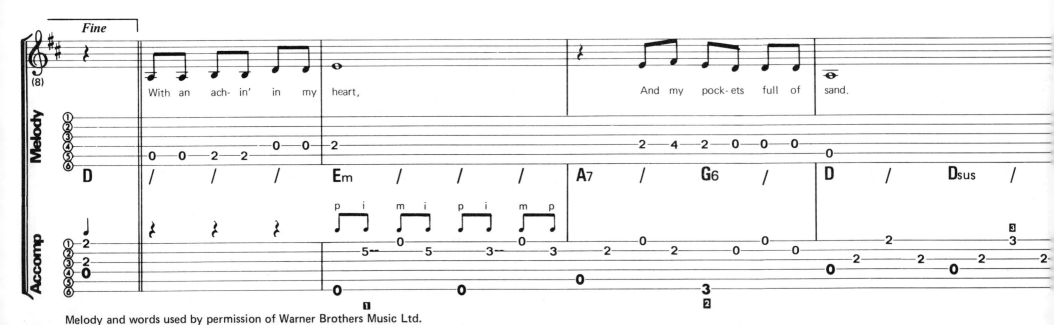

Melody and words used by permission of Warner Brothers Music Ltd.

In the early mornin' rain,
With a dollar in my hand,
With an achin' in my heart,
And my pockets full of sand.
I'm a long way from home
And I miss my loved one so.
In the early mornin' rain,
And no place to go.

3: Hear the mighty engines roar,
See the silver bird on high,
She's away and westward bound
Far above the clouds she'll fly,
Where the mornin' rain don't fall
And the sun always shines,
She'll be flyin' o'er my home
In about three hours time.

Out on runway number nine
Big seven-o-seven set to go,
Well, I'm standin' on the grass
Where the cold wind blows.
Well, the liquor tasted good
And the women all were fast,
Well, there she goes, my friend,
There she's rollin' now at last.

4: Well, this old airport's got me down,
It's no earthly good to me,
'Cause I'm stuck here on the ground
As cold and drunk as I can be.
You can't jump a jet plane
Like you can a freight train,
So I best be on my way
In the early mornin' rain.

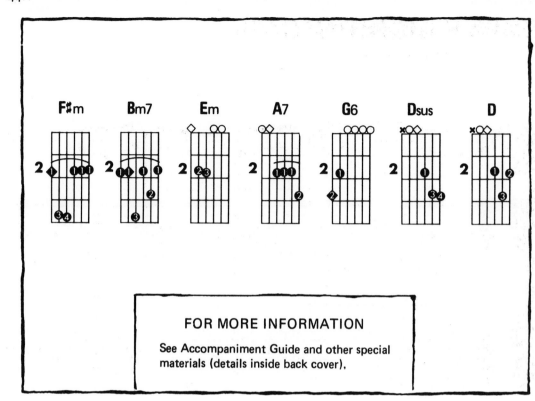

FOR MORE INFORMATION

See Accompaniment Guide and other special
materials (details inside back cover).

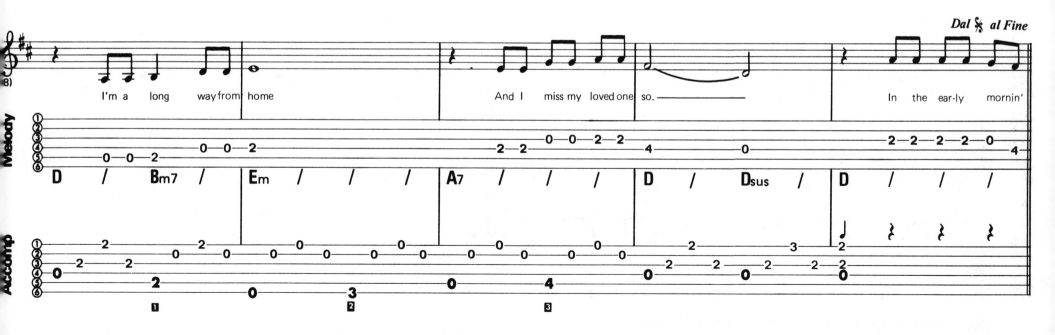

DRINK TO ME ONLY

Melody and accompaniment **1** (tablature)

Melody: Tradition
Words: Ben Jonson

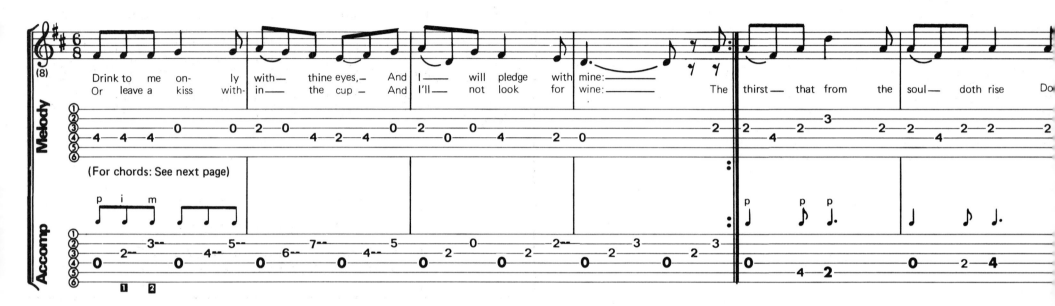

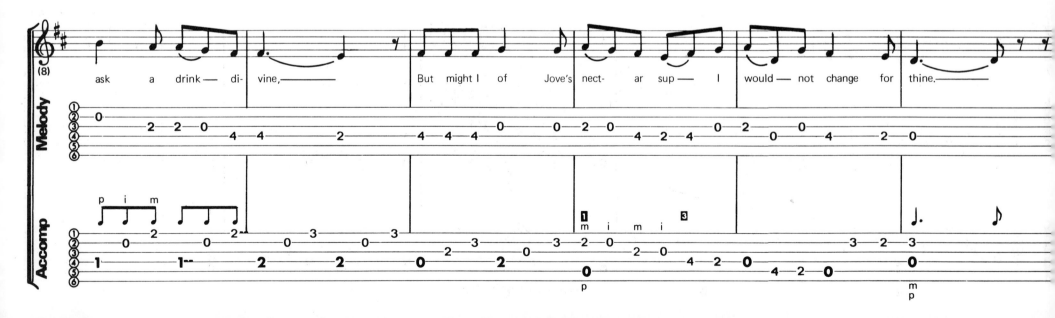

Barré- & open chords

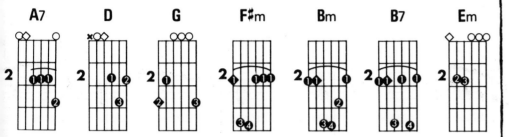

A7   D   G   F#m   Bm   B7   Em

FOR MORE INFORMATION

See Accompaniment Guide and other special materials (details inside back cover).

Drink to me only with thine eyes,
And I will pledge with mine:
Or leave a kiss within the cup
And I'll not look for wine:
The thirst that from the soul doth rise
Doth ask a drink divine,
But might I of Jov's nectar sup
I would not change for thine.

I sent thee late a rosy wreath,
Not so much honouring thee
As giving it a hope that there
It could not wither'd be:
But thou thereon didst only breathe,
And sendst it back to me,
Since when it grows, and smells, I swear,
Not of itself but thee.

DRINK TO ME ONLY
Accompaniment 2 (chords)

— Extra marks, to help you divide up the text

6/8

‖: D / / | G / / | B7 / / | Em / / |
Drink to----me--on——ly---with——thine eyes,——And
Or----leave a----kiss-----with- in------- the--cup-----And

| D / / | G D / | A7 | D / / / / :‖
I---------- will--pledge----with- mine:------------
I'll-------- not--look------for-- wine:- — — — — — —The

| D / / | Bm / / | D / / | F#m / / |
thirst-----that-- from-----the --soul------doth-rise-----Doth

| B7 / / / / / | Em / / / / / |
ask------- a-----drink------ di——vine,------------

| D / / | G / / | B7 / / | Em / / |
But might I-----of-------Jove's nect——ar---sup-------‖

| D / / | G D / | A7 | D / / / / :‖
would----- not---change-----for--- thine. ------------

THE SHADOW OF YOUR SMILE

Melody: Johnny Man[...]
Words: P.F. Webster

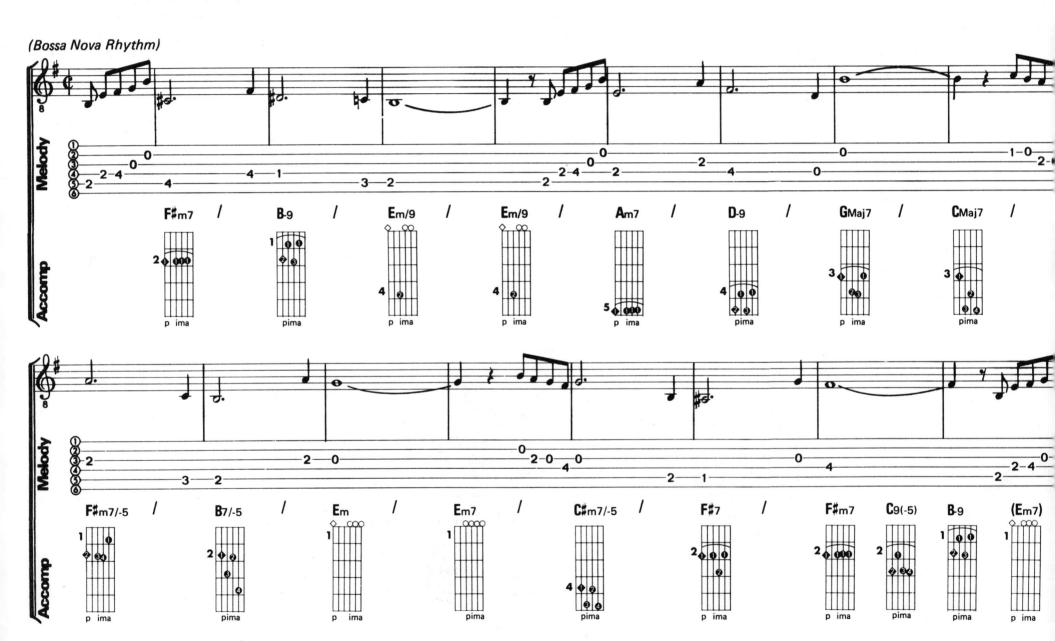

Melody and words used by permission of United Artists Music Ltd.

FOR MORE INFORMATION

See Accompaniment Guide and other special materials (details inside back cover).

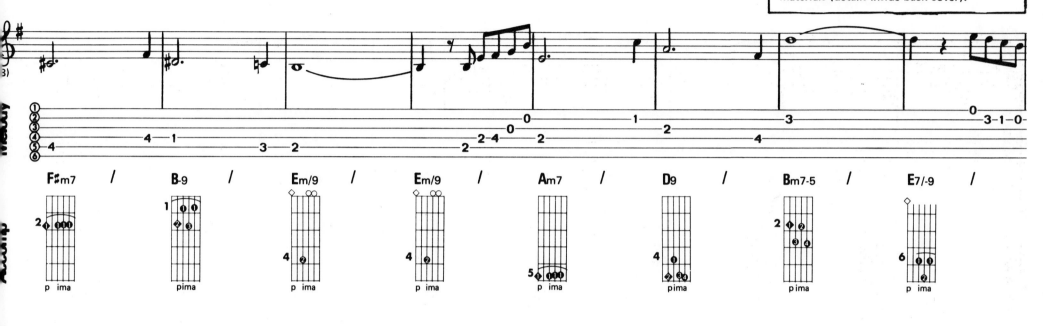

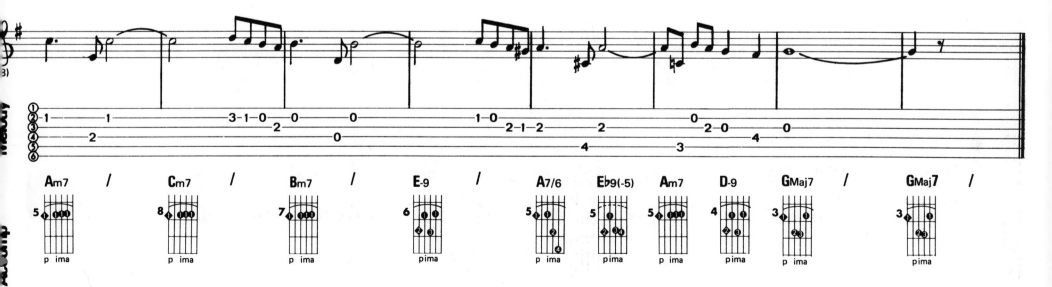

DARLING NELLY GREY

Melody and words: Tradition[al]

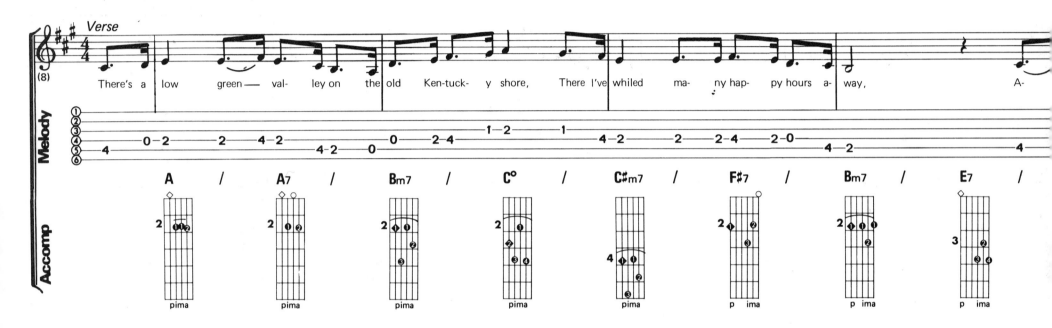

There's a low green — val- ley on the old Ken-tuck- y shore, There I've whiled ma- ny hap- py hours a- way, A-

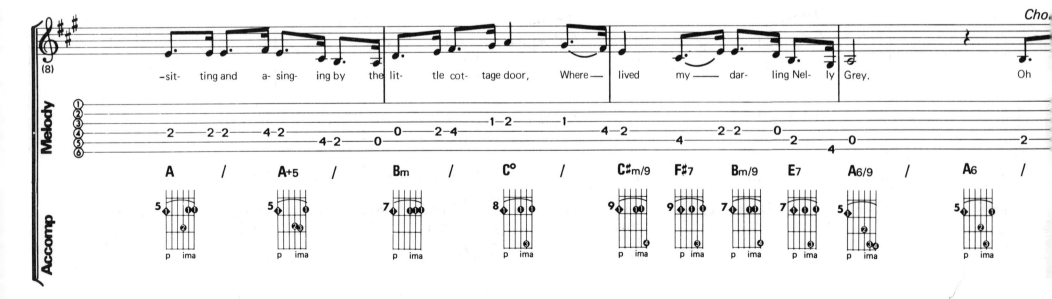

-sit- ting and a- sing- ing by the lit- tle cot- tage door, Where — lived my — dar- ling Nel- ly Grey. Oh